A TWISTER OF TWISTS, A TANGLER OF TONGUES

A TWISTER OF TWISTS, A TANGLER OF TONGUES

TONGUE TWISTERS COLLECTED BY ALVIN SCHWARTZ ILLUSTRATED BY GLEN ROUNDS

ANDRE DEUTSCH

First published 1974 by
André Deutsch Limited
105 Great Russell Street London wc1

Printed in Great Britain by
A. Wheaton & Co., Exeter

Paperback ISBN 0 233 96546 7
Hardback ISBN 0 233 96545 9

FOR BETSY

CONTENTS

PEGGY BABCOCK AND PETER PIPER

One of the hardest tongue twisters in the English language is "Peggy Babcock." Try to say it five times as fast as you can. If you are like most people I know, your tongue won't cooperate.

Every tongue twister is designed to tangle a tongue. But many of the longer twisters also are good stories. One of the funniest in this book is about a seller of saddles named Sam Short and his love affair with Sophia Sophronia Spriggs. It consists of over three hundred words, each of which starts with the letter *s*. Of course, the best a sensible person can do with such a twister is to read it aloud once, then give his tongue a rest.

Tongue twisters exist for the fun of it. But over the years they also have served other purposes. They have been used to train radio announcers, to test actors, to help with problems in speech, and to cure hiccups. (The prescription: repeat one medium-length twister five times while holding your breath.) At least one opera singer sang tongue twisters as part of her daily practice. And at least one dentist used them to test his patients' speech after he installed their new false teeth.

9

Perhaps the most exciting use ever made of a tongue twister occurred during World War II after Germany conquered Poland. Those Poles who continued to fight went into hiding. As a password they used a twister that someone who was not Polish would have great difficulty in pronouncing correctly. It was "Chrązaszcz brzmi w trzcinie," which sounds something like "Ch*ahn*-shcht bzhm*ee* ftsch*ee*-neeieh" and means "The beetle buzzes in the thicket."

The tongue twister about Sam Short was written in the 1890's by Katie Wheeler. But the persons responsible for our twisters usually are not known. Only their work survives, passing by word of mouth (at times with the help of an author) from one generation to the next.

In the process some twisters change. The famed Betty Botter, for example, now also is known as Betty Butter, Betty Botta, Betsy Butter, and just plain Betty. Moreover, a half dozen versions of her problem with bitter butter have come into use. In the southwestern United States, meanwhile, Peter Piper, the ancient pickled pepper picker, now has a companion, a prickly prangly pear picker named Peter Prangle.

The Peter Piper twister is one of the oldest in our folklore. It has been traced to an English grammar published in London in 1674, but Peter probably was roaming the streets even earlier. However, new twisters continue to appear, and by some mysterious process the best take root and spread.

This collection includes twisters on rockets, biscuit mixers, rubber baby buggy bumpers, Yo-Yo's, aluminum, preshrunk shirts, and other modern inventions, each the creation of an unknown author who had discovered the pleasure of fooling with words. Later in this book you can learn how to twist your own twisters, but now try some that already are part of our heritage.

Alvin Schwartz

Princeton, New Jersey

A TWISTER OF TWISTS,
　　Once twisted a twist,
And the twist that he twisted,
　　Was a three-twisted twist.
Now in twisting this twist,
　　If a twist should untwist,
The twist that untwisted
　　Would untwist the twist.

A TWISTER OF TWISTS,
A TANGLER OF TONGUES

ANIMALS
AND INSECTS

As the roaring rocket rose,
the restless roosters rollicked.

A noisy noise annoys an oyster.

Cows graze in groves on grass
which grows in grooves in groves.

The big black-backed bumblebee.

A critical cricket critic.

4 fat dogs frying fritters and
fiddling ferociously.

5 French friars fanning a fainted flea.

6 slippery seals slipping silently ashore.

6 silent snakes slithering slowly southward.

6 selfish shellfish.

8 gray geese grazing gaily into Greece.

66 sickly chicks.

The rat ran by the river with a lump of raw liver.

Black bug's blood.

The skunk sat on a stump and thunk
the stump stunk.
But the stump thunk the skunk stunk.

A skunk jumped over a stump in a skunk hole.

Once upon a barren moor
    There dwelt a bear,

also a boar.

The bear could not bear the boar,
    The boar thought the bear a bore.
At last the bear could bear no more
    That boar that bored him on the moor.
And so one morn he bored the boar—

    That boar will bore the bear no more.

A tree toad loved a she-toad
   That lived up in a tree.
She was a three-toed tree toad,
   But a two-toed toad was he.
The two-toed toad tried to win
   The she-toad's friendly nod,
For the two-toed toad loved the ground
   On which the three-toed toad trod.
But no matter how the two-toed tree toad tried,
   He could not please her whim.
In her tree-toad bower,
   With her three-toed power,
The she-toad vetoed him.

A pale pink proud peacock
pompously preened its pretty plumage.

Swan, swim over the sea.
Swim, swan, swim!
Swan, swim back again.
Well swum, swan!

My dame hath a lame tame crane.
My dame hath a crane that is lame.
Pray, gentle Jane, let my dame's tame crane
Feed and come home again.

The sixth sheik's sixth sheep's sick.

Sheep shouldn't sleep in a shack.
Sheep should sleep in a shed.

The wild wolf roams the wintry wastes.

A shy little she said, "Shoo!"
To a fly and a flea in a flue.

Pete's pa, Pete, poked to the pea patch to pick a peck of peas for the poor pink pig in the pine hole pig pen.

If a woodchuck could chuck wood,
　How much wood would a woodchuck chuck,
If a woodchuck could chuck wood?
　He would chuck, he would, as much as he
　could,
If a woodchuck could chuck wood.

Can you imagine

an imaginary

menagerie manager

imagining

managing

an imaginary

menagerie

?

FIGHTING MEN

Brisk brave brigadiers brandished broad bright blades, blunderbusses, and bludgeons.

Shining
soldiers.

Soldiers' shoulders s h u d d e r

when S H R I L L

shells *S H R I E K.*

Sister Susie's
sewing shirts
for soldiers.

Six twin-screw cruisers.

Seventy shuddering sailors
standing silent
as
short,
sharp,
shattering
shocks
shake
their splendid ship.

Naughty Nettie's knitting knotted nighties
for the Navy.

Ned Nott was shot
  and Sam Shott was not.
So it is better to be Shott
  than Nott.
Some say Nott
  was not shot.
But Shott says
  he shot Nott.
Either the shot Shott shot at Nott
  was not shot,
    or
  Nott was shot.
If the shot Shott shot shot Nott,
  Nott was shot.
But if the shot Shott shot shot Shott,
  then Shott was shot,
    not Nott.
However,
  the shot Shott shot shot not Shott—
  but Nott.

Mr. See owned a saw
   And Mr. Soar owned a seesaw.
Now See's saw sawed Soar's seesaw
   Before Soar saw See
Which made Soar sore.
   Had Soar seen See's saw
Before See sawed Soar's seesaw,
   See's saw would not have sawed
Soar's seesaw.
   So See's saw sawed Soar's seesaw.
But it was a shame to see Soar so sore
   Just because See's saw sawed
Soar's seesaw.

Bandy-legg'd Borachio Mustachio Whiskerifusti-
cus, the Bald and Brave Bombandino of Bagdad,
helped Abomilique Bluebeard Bashaw of Babel-
mandel to beat down an abominable bumblebee at
Balsora.

35

FOOD AND DRINK

Cuthbert's custard.

Greek grapes.

A big blue bucket of blue blueberries.

A cup of coffee in a copper coffee pot.

Double bubble gum bubbles double.

Pure food for four pure mules.

Tuesday is stew day.
Stew day is Tuesday.

Frances Fowler's father fried five floundering
flounder for Frances Fowler's father's father.

I never smelled a smelt that smelled
as bad as that smelt smelled.

Lotty licks lollies lolling in the lobby.

Sly Sam sips Sally's soup.

Nine nimble noblemen nibble nuts.

Betty Botter
  bought some butter,
But, she said,
  the butter's bitter.
If I put it
  in my batter,
It will make
  my batter bitter.
But a bit
  of better butter—
That would make
  my batter better.
So she bought
  a bit of butter,
Better than
  her bitter butter.
And she put it
  in her batter,
And the batter
  was not bitter.
So 'twas better
  Betty Botter
Bought a bit
  of better butter.

A box of biscuits, a box of mixed biscuits,
and a biscuit mixer.

Richard gave Robin a rap in the ribs
for roasting his rabbit so rare.

Barbara burned the brown bread badly.

Coop up the cook!

HEALTH

Lemon

liniment.

If one doctor doctors another, does the doctor who doctors the doctor doctor the doctor the way the doctor he is doctoring doctors? Or does he doctor the doctor the way the doctor who doctors doctors?

Good blood, bad blood.

Theophilus Thistledown,
the successful thistle sifter,
in sifting a sieve of unsifted thistles,
thrust three thousand thistles
through the thick of his thumb.
If, then, Theophilus Thistledown,
the successful thistle sifter,
thrust three thousand thistles
through the thick of his thumb,
see that thou,
in sifting a sieve of thistles,
do not get the unsifted thistles
stuck in *thy* thumb.

LOVE AND MARRIAGE

I saw Esau kissing Kate.
I saw Esau, he saw me.
And she saw I saw Esau.

Tho' a kiss be amiss
   She who misses the kisses,
As Miss without kiss,
   May miss being Mrs.

Bisquick—Kiss quick!

Kiss her quickly!

Kiss her quicker!

A tall eastern girl named Short long loved a big Mr. Little. But Little, thinking little of Short, loved a little lass named Long. To belittle Long, Short announced *she* would marry Little before long. This caused Little to shortly marry Long.

To make a long story short, did tall Short love big Little less because Little loved little Long more?

SHREWD SIMON SHORT

Shrewd Simon Short sewed shoes. Seventeen summers saw Simon's small, shabby shop still standing, saw Simon's selfsame squeaking sign still swinging swiftly, specifying:

SIMON SHORT
Smithfield's Sole Surviving
SHOEMAKER
Shoes Soled   •   Sewed Superfinely

Simon's spouse, Sally Short, sewed sheets, stitched shirts, stuffed sofas.

Simon's stout sturdy sons—Stephen, Samuel, Saul, Silas—sold sundries. Stephen sold silks, satins, shawls. Samuel sold saddles, stirrups. Saul sold silver spoons, specialties. Silas sold Sally Short's stuffed sofas.

Simon's second son, Samuel, saw Sophia Sophronia Spriggs somewhere. Sweet, sensible, smart Sophia Sophronia Spriggs. Sam soon showed strange symptoms. Surprisingly, Sam sighed sorrowfully, sang several serenades slyly, sought Sophia Spriggs' society, seldom stood selling saddles.

Simon stormed, scowled severely, said, "Sam seems so silly singing such senseless songs."

"Softly," said sweet Sally. "Sam's smitten. Sam's spied some sweetheart."

"Smitten!" snarled Simon. "Scatterbrained simpleton! Sentimental, silly schoolboy!"

Sally sighed sadly. Summoning Sam, she spoke sympathizingly. "Sam," said she, "Sire* seems singularly snappish. So, Sonny, stop strolling streets so soberly, stop singing sly serenades. Sell saddles sensibly, Sam. See Sophia Sophronia Spriggs speedily."

"So soon?" said Sam, startled.

"So soon, surely," said Sally, smilingly, "specially since Sire shows such spirit."

So Sam, somewhat scared, sauntered slowly storeward, shaking stupendously. "Sophia Sophronia Spriggs ... Sam Short's spouse ... sounds splendid," said Sam softly.

Sam soon spied Sophia starching shirts, singing softly. Seeing Sam, she stopped, saluting Sam smilingly.

Sam stuttered shockingly. "Sp-sp-splendid s-s-summer s-s-season, So-So-Sophia."

"Somewhat sultry," suggested Sophia.

"S-s-sartin," said Sam.

"Still selling saddles, Sam?" said Sophia.

*An old-fashioned word for Father

"S-s-sartin," said Sam.

Silence, seventeen seconds.

"Sire shot sixteen snipe Saturday, Sam," said Sophia.

Silence, seventy-seven seconds.

"See sister Sue's sunflowers," said Sophia socially, stopping such stiff silence.

Such sprightly sauciness stimulated Sam strangely. So, swiftly speaking, Sam said, "Sue's sunflowers seem saying, 'Sophia Sophronia Spriggs, Samuel Short stroll serenely, seek some sparkling streams, sing some sweet, soul-stirring strain. . . .'"

Sophia snickered, so Sam stopped. She stood silently several seconds.

Said Sam, "Stop smiling, Sophia. Sam's seeking some sweet spouse!"

She still stood silently.

"Speak, Sophia, speak! Such silence speculates sorrow."

"Seek Sire Spriggs, Sam," said Sophia.

Sam sought Sire Spriggs.

Sire Spriggs said, "Sartin."

MUSIC

A tooter who tooted a flute
   Tried to tutor two tutors to toot.
Said the two to the tutor,
   "Is it harder to toot or
To tutor two tutors to toot?"

If to hoot and to toot
   A Hottentot tot
Was taught by a Hottentot tutor,
   Should the tutor get hot
If the Hottentot tot
   Hoots and toots
At the Hottentot tutor?

While trying to whistle

Christopher Twistle

twisted his tongue.

Quinn's twin sisters sing tongue twisters.

This is a zither.

NATURE

This thistle seems like that thistle.

3 tree twigs.

6 slim saplings.

6 thick swamps.

6 thin thistle sticks.

Really rural.

Beautiful
b a b b l i n g
brooks
b u b b l e
between
blossoming
banks.

Georgia's gorge is gorgeous.

The seething sea ceaseth seething.

Some shun sunshine.

OCCUPATIONS

Peter Piper picked a peck of pickled pepper.
  A peck of pickled pepper Peter Piper picked.
If Peter Piper picked a peck of pickled pepper,
  Where is the peck of pickled pepper
Peter Piper picked?

A bootblack blacks boots
with a black blacking brush.

Six silly sisters sell silk to six sickly seniors.

Bonnie Bliss blows big beautiful blue bubbles.

Who will wet the whetstone
while Willie whistles wistfully?

Slim Sam shaved six slippery chins
in six seconds.

Old, oily Ollie oils oily autos.

She stood at the door of Mrs. Smith's fish sauce shop welcoming him in.

Sally's selfish selling shellfish,
So Sally's shellfish seldom sell.

The sun shines on shop signs.

Flocking shoppers shopping.

If neither he sells seashells,
Nor she sells seashells,
Who shall sell seashells?
Shall
seashells
be
sold
?

Wise
wives
whistle
while
weaving
worsted
waistcoats.

She says she shall sew a sheet.

She sewed shirts seriously.

Rush the washing, Russell!

65

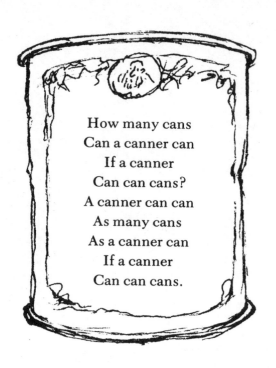

How many cans
Can a canner can
If a canner
Can can cans?
A canner can can
As many cans
As a canner can
If a canner
Can can cans.

A conversation between a woman who has left some pots to be mended and the repairman:

"Are you copper bottoming 'um, my man?"
"No, I'm aluminuming 'um, mum."

Esaw Wood sawed wood. Esaw Wood would saw wood. Oh, the wood that Wood would saw! One day Esaw Wood saw a saw saw wood as no other wood-saw Wood ever saw would saw wood. Of *all* the wood-saws Wood ever saw saw wood, Wood never saw a wood-saw that would saw like the wood-saw Wood saw would.

Now Esaw saws with that saw he saw saw wood.

Wood said he would carry the wood

through the wood.

And if Wood said he would,

Wood would.

Shave a cedar shingle thin.

A maid with a duster
　　Made a furious bluster
Dusting a bust in the hall.
　　When the bust it was dusted
The bust it was busted,
　　The bust it was dust, that's all.

A lively young fisher named Fischer
　　Fished for fish from the edge of a fissure.
A fish with a grin
　　Pulled the fisherman in!
Now they are hunting the fissure
　　For Fischer.

A regal rural ruler.

OVERWEAR
AND UNDERWEAR

W H O
washed Washington's
white woolen underwear
when Washington's washerwoman went West?

His shirt soon shrank in the suds.

Preshrunk shirts.

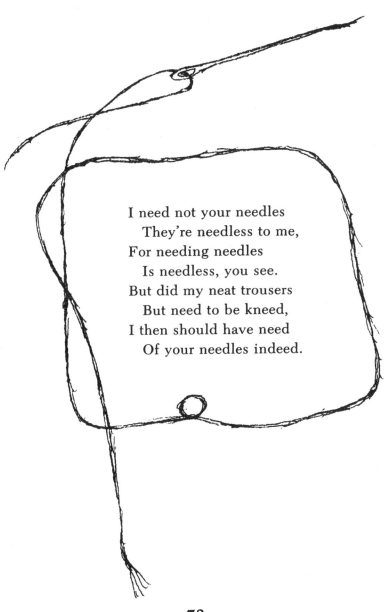

I need not your needles
  They're needless to me,
For needing needles
  Is needless, you see.
But did my neat trousers
  But need to be kneed,
I then should have need
  Of your needles indeed.

Does this shop stock short socks with spots?

Sara saw a sash shop full of showy, shiny sashes.

Shipshape suit shops ship shapely suits.

Shoes and socks shock Susie.

PEOPLE, WITCHES, GHOSTS

Is there a pleasant peasant present?

Peggy Babcock.

Tim, the thin twin tinsmith.

Wheedling, weeping Winnie

wails W I L D L Y.

Which is the witch that wished the wicked wish?

Did you do it? Don't do it!

Babbling Bert blamed Bess.

As I went into the garden
  I saw five brave maids
Sitting on five broad beds
  Braiding broad braids.
I said to these five brave maids
  Sitting on five broad beds
Braiding broad braids,
  "Braid broad braids, brave maids."

Shy Sheila shakes soft shimmering silks.

79

Round and round the rugged rock the ragged
rascal ran.

Amidst the mists and coldest frosts
    With barest wrists and stoutest boasts
He thrusts his fists against the posts
    But still insists he sees the ghosts.

I thought a thought.

But the thought I thought wasn't the thought I thought I thought.

If the thought I thought I thought had been the thought I thought, I wouldn't have thought so much.

READING,
WRITING,
ARITHMETIC

I can't stand

rotten writin'

when it's written rotten.

The bootblack brought the book back.

Literally literary literature.

Blame the big bleak black book!

'Lisbeth lisps lengthy lessons.

Thrice times three,
Twice times two.

A queer quick questioning quiz.

Miss Smith dismisseth us.

TRAVEL

Cheap ship trips.

A ship saileth south soon.

The

sinking

steamer

sunk.

The two twenty-two tore through town.

Cross crossings cautiously!

He ran from the Indies
to the Andes in his undies.

I go by a Blue Goose bus.

Let little Nellie run a little.

Don't run along the wrong lane!

Slim Sam slid sideways.

Unique New York.

The dude dropped in at the Dewdrop Inn.

OTHER THINGS

Rubber baby buggy bumpers.

Toy boat.

Silver thimbles.

Yellow Yo-Yo's.

Thin sticks, thick bricks.

A black-backed bath brush.

A lump of red leather, a red leather lump.

Red leather, yellow leather.

A knapsack strap.

My wife gave Mr. Snipe's
wife's knife a swipe.

Tom threw Tim three thumbtacks.

I never felt felt that felt
like that felt felt.

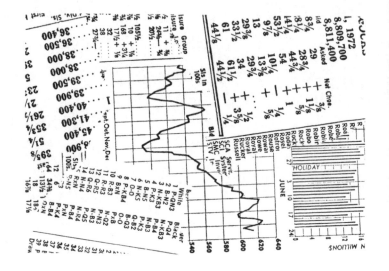

Strange strategic statistics.

Truly plural.

96

Does
the
wristwatch
shop
shut
soon
?

Which wristwatches
are Swiss wristwatches?

When does the wristwatch strap shop shut?

The wild wind whipped Whit from the wharf.

We surely shall see the sun shine soon.

TWISTERS IN
OTHER TONGUES

Man speaks in almost three thousand languages, and in almost every one there are tongue twisters. In Spanish the word for tongue twister is *trabalengua,* which is pronounced "tra-ba-*len-gwa*" and means "troubled tongue." This section contains "tongue troublers" from nine languages. Their sounds are translated into English sounds so that if you don't speak a particular language you still can enjoy the trouble.

FRENCH

Diderot dînait du dos d'un dodo dindon.

Dee-de-*ro* dee-nay du dough *du*n doh-*doh* dahn-*don.*

Diderot dined on the back of a plump turkey.

Le ver vert va vers le verre vert.

Le vhere vhere va vhere le vhere vhere.

The green grub goes to the green grass.

Six sous ces saucissons-ci?!

See soo say so-see-son-see?!

Six cents for these sausages?!

GERMAN

Fischers Fritz fischt frische Fische.
Frische Fische fischt Fischers Fritz.

Fishers Fritz fisht *frish*-eh *fish*-eh.
Frish-eh *fish*-eh fisht Fischers Fritz.

Fritz Fischer fishes for fresh fish.
Fresh fish fish for Fritz Fischer.

GREEK

Mia πaπia ma πia πaπia?

Mi-a *papi*-a ma *pi*-a *papi*-a?

One duck, but which duck?

102

HEBREW

שרה שרה שיר שמח

Sah-ra *sha*-rah sheerrr *sa*-mayach.

Sarah sings a happy song.

HUNGARIAN

Mit sütsz kis szücs, sós húst? Sütsz kis szücs?

Mit sheuts kish seuch, shosh hoosht? Sheuts kish seuch?

What are you roasting, little hunter? Are you roasting salt meat?

ITALIAN

Paolo, pittore poco pratico, pinse pillole per poco prezzo.

Paw-lo, pit-*to*-rey *poko* *pra*-tico, *pin*-sey *pil*-lo-ley per *poko* *pret*-zo.

Paul, an inexperienced painter, painted pills cheaply.

Un limon, mezzo limon.

Oon lee-*mon*, medzo lee-*mon*.

One lemon, half a lemon.

JAPANESE

生むぎ　生ごめ　生たまご

Na*ma*-mugi, na*ma*-gome, na*ma*-tamago.

Raw wheat, raw rice, raw eggs.

POLISH

Nie pieprz wieprza pieprzem.

Nyeh pey-*ep*sch vey-*ep*-shah pey-*ep*-schem.

Do not pepper the hog with pepper.

SPANISH

Yo no compro coco. Porque como poco coco, poco coco compro.

Yo no *kom*-pro *koko*. Por-*kay* *komo* *poko* *koko*, *poko* *koko* *kom*-pro.

I do not buy coconut. Since I eat little coconut, I buy little coconut.

Mi ma*ma* me mima mucho.

Me ma*ma* me *mee*-ma *moo*-cho.

My mother spoils me a lot.

Tres tristes tigres trillaron trigo en un trigal.

Tray *tree*-stays *tee*-grres tree-*ya*rron *tree*-go en un tree-*gal*.

Three sad tigers threshing wheat in a wheat field.

Compre poco capa parda, porque el que poco capa parda compra poco capa parda paga.

Kom-prey *p*oko *ka*-pah *par*-dah, pour-*kay* el keh *p*oko *ka*-pah *par*-dah *kom*-prah *p*oko *ka*-pah *par*-dah *pa*-gah.

Buy only a little brown cape, for he who buys only a little brown cape pays only for a little brown cape.

El otorrinolaringologo de Parangaricutirimicuaro
se quiere
desotorrinolaringologoparangaricutirimicuarizar
porque si no se
desotorrinolaringologoparangaricutirimicuarizara
lo van a
desotorrinolaringologoparangaricutirimicuarizar.

El oto-*ree*-no-*lah*-rine-*go*-logo deh Paran-*gah*-ree-
   coo-*tee*-*ree*-mi-*quah*-ro
sey *key*ai-reh
des-oto-*ree*-no-*lah*-rine-*go*-logo-paran-*gah*-ree-coo-
   tee-*ree*-mi-*quah*-ree-*zar*
pour-*kay* see no sey
des-oto-*ree*-no-*lah*-rine-*go*-logo-paran-*gah*-ree-coo-
   tee-*ree*-mi-*quah*-ree-*zara*
low vahn a
des-oto-*ree*-no-*lah*-rine-*go*-logo-paran-*gah*-ree-coo-
   tee-*ree*-mi-*quah*-ree-*zar.*

The eye-ear-nose-throat doctor in Parangaricutirimicuaro
wishes
to stop practicing in Parangaricutirimicuaro
because if he doesn't
stop practicing in Parangaricutirimicuaro
they will make him
stop practicing in Parangaricutirimicuaro.

TO TWIST YOUR OWN TWISTER

The best way to begin is by writing several senseless sentences whose words each start with the same sound or the same letter. For example: Fearless, foolish, friendly Frank Farrington faints fast on Fridays. Just write down what occurs to you. If you follow the rule you should tangle a tongue.

As you become experienced try using two different sounds. Throughout this book there are many such combinations which can make a twister even more frustrating. In "*Slim Sam slid sideways*," the *s* and the *sl* are the trap. In "*She sells seashells* by the *seashore*," it is the *s* and the *sh*. In "*Black bug's blood*," it is the *bl* and the *bu*.

You also can play a tongue-twister game. Only one other player is needed. Each of you makes up a twister. Then each, in turn, repeats the other's twister five times as fast as he can. If either of you stumbles, he loses. But if both of you do, or neither, the game goes on with another pair of twisters and another test of skill.

NOTES,
SOURCES,
BIBLIOGRAPHY

NOTES

A *Twister of twists* (page 13). The "Twister" twister, from which the title of this book is taken, is one of the oldest in the English language. However, it has changed considerably since it appeared in 1674 in *Grammatica Linguae Anglicanae* by John Wallis, a grammar published in Oxford, England. Then it read:

> When a Twister, a-twisting, will twist him a twist;/ For the twisting of his twist, he three times doth intwist;/ But, if one of the twists of the twist do untwist,/ The twine that untwisteth, untwisteth the twist.
> Untwirling the twine that untwisteth between,/ He twirls, with his twister, the two in a twine;/ Then, twice having twisted the twines of the twine,/ He twisteth, the twine he has twined, in twain.
> The twain that, in twining, before in the twine;/ As twins were untwisted, he now doth untwine;/ Twixt the twain intertwisting a twine more between,/ He, twirling his twister, makes a twist of the twine.

Sister Susie's sewing shirts for soldiers (page 31): The "Sister Susie" twister actually is part of a song that was popular in England during World War I. Whether the twister or the song came first is not known, but the entire song was a twister of sorts. Sidney Hamer of Washington, D.C., who was a performer in English music halls in that period, recalled these lyrics in a letter to the Library of Congress:

> Sister Susie's sewing shirts for soldiers./ Such saucy, soft, short shirts our shy young sister Susie sews;/ Some soldiers send epistles, say they'd sooner sleep on thistles/ Than the saucy, soft, short shirts our shy, young sister Susie sews.

Shrewd Simon sewed shoes (page 50): As noted in the introduction, the twister about Simon, Sally, and Sam Short was created in the 1890's by Katie L. Wheeler. She called it "Sam Short's Sparkin'," or Sam Short's courting. The complete version of the "Sam Short" twister contains 418 words, each starting with the letter *s*. To keep the twister to a practical length for this book, the original was shortened somewhat. But even in its abridged form, it is a remarkable work. The complete twister resides in the Folk Song Section of the Library of Congress. It was contributed to the library in 1954 by Katie Wheeler's son, Carlton L. Wheeler of Penn Yan, New York.

The seething sea ceaseth seething (page 58): This is a variation of one of the most durable twisters in the United States. The best known version is "The sea ceaseth and it sufficeth for us," which some believe to be of Biblical origin. In the *Standard Dictionary of Folk-*

lore, Mythology, and Legend, the folklorist Charles Francis Potter suggests that the twister might have its roots in the Old Testament's book of Jonah, "the sea ceased from her raging" and the New Testament's Gospel of Saint John, "Lord, show us the Father, and it sufficeth us."

Peter Piper picked a peck of pickled pepper (page 60): The "Peter Piper" twister is without doubt the best known of our tongue tanglers. It also is among the most ancient, having appeared with the "Twister" twister in *Grammatica Linguae Anglicanae,* the grammar referred to earlier which was published in 1674. It is one of some two dozen twisters which make up an early but undated pamphlet, *Peter Piper's Practical Principles of Plain and Perfect Pronunciation.* In addition to Peter Piper, these tell in alphabetical order of a weird collection of characters, from Andrew Airpump to Walter Waddle.

Each twister follows the same pattern: a statement ("Peter Piper picked a peck of pickled pepper"); a question ("Did Peter Piper pick a peck of pickled pepper?"); a second question expressing doubt about the assumed answer to the first ("If Peter Piper picked a peck of pickled pepper, where's the peck of pickled pepper Peter Piper picked?"). Here, for example, is the report on Questing Quidnunc:

Questing Quidnunc quizzed a queerish question./ Did Questing Quidnunc quiz a queerish question?/ If Questing Quidnunc quizzed a

queerish question, what's the queerish question Questing Quidnunc quizzed?

*She stood at the door of Mrs. Smith's fish sauce shop
welcoming him in* (page 63): This version of the "fish
sauce" twister is from the United States and Canada. In
England, a Mrs. Burgess rather than a Mrs. Smith
operates the fish sauce shop.

Sally's selfish selling shellfish (page 63): This is but
one of a score of variations of the famous twister "She
sells seashells by the seashore," all of which rely on the
s-sh trap.

Amidst the mists and coldest frosts (page 80): No one
has demonstrated conclusively what the "mists and
frosts" twister means, but there have been several explan-
ations. Perhaps the most logical is offered by Charles
Francis Potter, in the *Standard Dictionary of Folklore,
Mythology, and Legend,* who reports that during the nine-
teenth century in New England the twister was known as
"The Drunken Saylor." At least one version starts with
"Round and round the rock the ragged rascal ran," which
frequently is treated as a twister in its own right.

SOURCES

A number of tongue twisters in this book were recalled from my childhood. Some were acquired from friends and acquaintances. As word of my project spread, others were sent to me by persons I did not know but who had twisters they wanted to share. Among these, the major contributor was Wallace G. Scott, a California speech teacher. In addition, the following folklore archives were important resources:

The Louis C. Johnson Archive at the New York State Historical Association, Cooperstown, New York. This collection was gathered in the 1940's by Professor Johnson's students at Albany State Teachers College (now Albany State College), Albany, New York. It was made available by Professor Bruce R. Buckley of the Cooperstown Graduate Programs, and Mrs. Marion Brophey, librarian in charge of special collections.

The Old Sturbridge Village Archive, Sturbridge, Massachusetts, directed by Roger C. Parks.

The University of Pennsylvania Folklore Archive, Philadelphia, Pennsylvania, directed by Professor Dan Ben-Amos.

The Folk Song Section of the Library of Congress, Washington, D. C. One resource here was the massive WPA Folklore Archive assembled on a state-by-state basis during the great economic depression in the 1930's. The collectors were unemployed folklorists and writers the government hired as part of the Federal Writers Project. Another resource was material assembled early in the 1950's by Duncan Emrich, then chief folklorist at the library, who conducted a nationwide radio program in which he asked his listeners to contribute folklore on various subjects, including tongue twisters. "Sam Short's Sparkin'" came to the library through this program. My guide in this aspect of my research was Joseph C. Hickerson, reference librarian in the Folk Song Section.

Another important resource was Professor Kenneth Goldstein of the University of Pennsylvania who placed at my disposal his extensive personal library of folklore.

Twisters in languages other than English were provided by Professors Valentine T. Bill, J. A. Baer, Paul Cucchi, Andras Hamori, Mantaro J. Hashimoto, and Edwin A. Hopkins of Princeton University, Princeton, New Jersey; Ronald Gendaszek, Herbert Hagens, and Manuel Morales of Princeton High School; Roslyn Staras, principal of the Hebrew school at the Princeton Jewish Center; Professor Manuel Ramos of Hostos Community College, Bronx, New York; Panayotis G. Pyrpyris of the New School for Social Research, New York; Emmanuel Hatziemmanuel of the Greek Orthodox Archdiocese of North and South America, New York; and Elsa Granade, Sing Gong Liu, and Stanley Pashko of Princeton, New Jersey.

BIBLIOGRAPHY

BOOKS

Books of particular interest to young people are marked with an asterisk (*).

Baring-Gould, William S. and Ceil, *The Annotated Mother Goose.* New York, Clarkson N. Potter, 1962.
Bell's Standard Elocutionist. London, William Mullen & Son, 1878.
*Botkin, Benjamin A., and Withers, Carl A., *The Illustrated Book of American Folklore.* New York, Grosset & Dunlap, 1958.
Botkin, Benjamin A., *Treasury of American Folklore.* New York, Crown Publishers, 1944.
Brewster, Paul G., "Children's Games and Rhymes," *Frank C. Brown Collection of North Carolina Folklore,* V. 1. Durham, N.C., Duke University Press, 1952.
*Emrich, Duncan, *The Nonsense Book.* New York, Four Winds Press, 1970.
*Emrich, Marian V., and Korson, George C., *The Child's Book of Folklore.* New York, Dial Press, 1947.
*Halliwell-Phillips, James Orchard, *The Nursery Rhymes and Nursery Tales of England.* London, Frederick Warne and Co., 1865.

Howard, Dorothy, *Folk Rhymes and Jingles of American Children*. New York, New York University, 1938. Unpublished doctoral dissertation.

Hyatt, Harry M., *Folklore from Adams County, Illinois*. New York, Alma Egan Hyatt Foundation, 1935.

*Justus, May T., *The Complete Peddler's Pack: Games, Songs, Rhymes, & Riddles from Mountain Folklore*. Knoxville, Tennessee, University of Tennessee Press, 1967.

Koch, William E., and Sacket, Sidney J., *Kansas Folklore*. Lincoln, Nebraska, University of Nebraska Press, 1961.

Opie, Iona and Peter, *I Saw Esau: Traditional Rhymes of Youth*. London, Williams & Norgate, 1947.

————, *The Lore and Language of School Children*. London and New York, Oxford University Press, 1959.

————, *The Oxford Dictionary of Nursery Rhymes*. London and New York, Oxford University Press, 1951.

————, *The Oxford Nursery Rhyme Book*. London and New York, Oxford University Press, 1955.

Parkin, Ken, *Anthology of British Tongue Twisters*. London, Samuel French, 1969.

Peter Piper's Practical Principles of Plain and Perfect Pronunciation. London, J. Harris, undated.

*Potter, Charles Francis, *More Tongue Tanglers & a Rigmarole*. Cleveland and New York, World Publishing Company, 1964.

*————, *Tongue Tanglers.* Cleveland and New York, World Publishing Company, 1962.

*Withers, Carl A., *A Rocket in My Pocket: The Rhymes and Chants of Young Americans.* New York, Holt, Rinehart, & Winston, 1948.

*————, *Treasury of Games, Riddles, Stunts, Tricks, Tongue-Twisters, Rhymes, Chanting, Singing.* New York, Grosset & Dunlap, 1969.

Wallis, John, *Grammatica Linguae Anglicanae.* Oxford, England, 1674.

ARTICLES

Cansler, Loman D., "Midwestern and British Children's Lore Compared." *Western Folklore,* v.27:1 (1968).

Emrich, Duncan, "The Ancient Game of Tongue Twisters." *American Heritage,* February, 1955, p. 119.

The Golden Era, San Francisco: v.5-17 (1857-68).

Gordon, Maxine W., "The Folklore of Vieques, Yauco, and Loqvillo, Puerto Rico." *Journal of American Folklore,* v.64:55 (1951).

Leland, Charles E., "Possible Origin of a Nursery Rhyme." *Journal of American Folklore,* v.4:170 (1891). The possibility, later disproved, that the name Peter Piper derives from Peter Pipernus, a seventeenth-century Italian author and priest.

Leventhal, Nancy C., and Cray, Ed, "Depth Collecting from a Sixth Grade Class." *Western Folklore,* v.22:159, 231 (1963).

Loomis, C. Grant, "A Handful of Tongue Twisters." *Western Folklore,* v.8:373 (1949).

Mook, Maurice A., "Tongue Tanglers from Western Pennsylvania." *Journal of American Folklore,* v.72:291 (1959).

O'Brien, Alice Crissman, "Tongue Twisters from California." *Western Folklore,* v.22:164 (1963).

Potter, Charles Francis, "Alphabet Rimes." *Standard Dictionary of Folklore, Mythology, and Legend,* v.1. New York, Funk & Wagnalls, 1949.

————, "Tongue Twisters." *Standard Dictionary of Folklore, Mythology, and Legend,* v.2. New York, Funk & Wagnalls, 1949.

Potts, John William, "Peter Piper's Proper Pronunciation of Perfect English versus Peter Pipernus." *Journal of American Folklore,* v.5:74 (1892).

Steadman, J. M., Jr., "Tongue-Twisters: Difficult Pronunciation as a Source of Verbal Taboos." *American Speech,* v.11:203 (1956).

"A Twist of Twisters." *New York Folklore Quarterly,* v.3:246 (1947).

Waugh, F. W., "Canadian Folklore from Ontario." *Journal of American Folklore,* v.31:4 (1918).

Winslow, David J., "An Annotated Collection of Children's Lore." *Keystone Folklore Quarterly,* v.11:151 (1966).

————, "An Introduction to Oral Tradition Among Children." *Keystone Folklore Quarterly,* v.11:43 (1966).

Wintemberg, W. J. and Katherine, "Folklore from Grey County, Ontario." *Journal of American Folklore,* v.31:82 (1918).

ABOUT ALVIN SCHWARTZ

Alvin Schwartz has written many books for young people and for families on subjects as varied as folklore, crafts, hobbies, museums, labor unions, and urban problems. He works in a tiny studio in Princeton, New Jersey, next to the house where he lives with his wife, four children, and two cats.

ABOUT GLEN ROUNDS

Glen Rounds spent his childhood on ranches in South Dakota and Montana. He attended art school in Kansas City, Missouri, and New York City, and now lives in Southern Pines, North Carolina. He has illustrated many books for young people.